Lovely, Dark and Deep

E. J. Myers

Lovely, Dark and Deep

E. J. Myers

Montemayor Press

Montpelier, Vermont

For information contact:

Montemayor Press
P. O. Box 546
Montpelier, VT 05601

Web site: www.MontemayorPress.com

1 3 5 7 9 10 8 6 4 2

Special thanks to Meredith Sue Willis for selecting this essay for publication in *Hamilton Stone Review,* Issue No. 36, Spring 2017. The digital version is available on the Web at:

http://www.hamiltonstone.org/hsr36nonfiction.html#myers

for Jim Barszcz

Lovely, Dark and Deep

E. J. Myers

Midway in the journey of our life
I came to myself in a dark wood . . .

    —Dante Alighieri, *Inferno* I 1-2 [1]

The property that my wife and I own in Vermont consists of ten acres: five of open land, five of forest. The open land covers most of the plot's high end, an acre of lawn surrounding the house and four acres of meadow rolling downward to the woods. A trust owns the large expanse of land to the south. Our wooded terrain declines further to the east and abuts another neighbor's forty- or fifty-acre plot. What's down in there delights us in many ways. The previous owners cleared brush and saplings to create hiking paths; there's a little stream along the northern property line; and the woods are dense enough that when we walk there, we quickly lose a sense of scale and imagine our snippet of forest to be large. What we own is actually a small property by local standards. With our neighbors' land unfenced and undeveloped, however, and with coyote, fox, deer, and moose footprints crisscrossing the snow all winter, the woods around us somehow feel expansive and wild.

During our second year of living in Vermont, Edith and I decided to contact Brooke and Donna, the couple who own the property to the south of ours. They had "posted" their land—that is, had put up signs warning against intrusion. State law requires people to contact the owners in writing before setting foot on posted land. Our request for permission received a cordial note in the mail: "We welcome our neighbors to enjoy exploring our little woods on foot year 'round. In the summertime the trail should make for a great hike to town."

Following this go-ahead, we started venturing deeper into the forest to reconnoiter. The month was February, the weather cold but less snowy than during our first winter. The snowpack was a crusty ten inches deep. Edith chose to use snowshoes, while I preferred to wear knee-high insulated boots. Together we headed due south from our property; we slogged until we hit a spur of the VAST Trail, a network of paths maintained by the statewide snowmobilers' club; and we then angled east over a hilltop until we hit the main path. From there the trail wound its way down to the farms bordering the roads below it. We had the woods to ourselves. We saw many animals' tracks in the snow but no sign of the animals themselves.

"You Will Be Fine"

This is the forest primeval.

—Henry Wadsworth Longfellow,
Evangeline, Canto I [2]

This is not the forest primeval. While inspiring illusions of being ancient, Vermont's woods are relatively new. European settlers in the 17th and 18th centuries clear-cut huge areas of the Northeast to create their farms; then, during the 19th century, as the frontier moved west and emigration started easing population pressures in New England, a process of natural reforestation began. This trend continued during the 20th century and into the 21st. Deep in our own woods, we have found agricultural machinery abandoned in what had been open farmland many decades earlier. Three fourths of Vermont's land is now forested; in its percentage of total surface area, this state is the fourth-most wooded in the nation. Our property is typical of this countryside. But because the process of reforestation is so recent, most of the trees here are small: maples thinner than the lodgepole pines of my Colorado youth. Old-growth maples, oaks, and other big trees are now uncommon.

Even so, the forest can feel ominous. Our neighbors Brooke and Donna warned us outright in their message: "Please be aware that a black bear has her den on our land, and there are numerous transient predators, including red fox, wolves, and coyotes. Exercise a degree of caution, and if you see them, give them their space, and you will be fine." All very reassuring. Even so, crossing paths with any of these animals face to face would be an encounter we choose to avoid. We see their footprints. We hear the coyotes' howls and yips at night. We keep our distance.

Stopping by Woods

"Friends who were present told me that after reading it, he looked up startled and said, 'Well, now, that does have a good deal of the ultimate about it, doesn't it?' Is it possible that he really had forgotten?"

—W. D. Snodgrass regarding Robert Frost's poem "Stopping by Woods on a Snowy Evening" [3]

n late June of 1922, after an entire night of writing at his kitchen table in the South Shaftsbury, Vermont, house where he lived with his family, Robert Frost realized that morning had dawned. "Having finished 'New Hampshire,'" Frost wrote later, "I went outdoors, got out sideways and didn't disturb anybody in the house, and about nine or ten o'clock went back in and wrote the piece about a snowy evening and the little horse as if I'd had an hallucination." This experience of "piggybacking" one poem on another wasn't unusual for Frost. "Sometimes one [poem] would grow out of an idea, leaving me relaxed. At other times the idea would produce a second growth, coercing itself as a Siamese twin on its predecessor . . . 'Stopping by Woods on a Snowy Evening' was written just about that way . . . But I must admit, it was written in a few minutes without any strain." [4] Frost immediately recognized that he had written something unusual. In a letter to

Louis Untermeyer, Frost described this poem as "my best bid for remembrance." "Stopping by Woods" received widespread acclaim following its publication in 1923, and it is arguably the best-known, best-loved of Frost's works.[5] Many generations of schoolchildren have read it in their English classes; countless mourners have heard its last lines quoted at funerals; millions of people have cherished it; and millions of others have mocked it for what they perceive as its picture-postcard sentiments.

Stopping by Woods on a Snowy Evening

Whose woods these are I think I know.
His house is in the village though;
He will not see me stopping here
To watch his woods fill up with snow.

My little horse must think it queer
To stop without a farmhouse near
Between the woods and frozen lake
The darkest evening of the year.

He gives his harness bells a shake
To ask if there is some mistake.
The only other sound's the sweep
Of easy wind and downy flake.

The woods are lovely, dark and deep.
But I have promises to keep,
And miles to go before I sleep,
And miles to go before I sleep. [6]

What has amused and puzzled me about "Stopping by Woods" ever since I first encountered it as a teenager has been the disparity between the poem's sunny reputation and its more fundamental, darker nature. This reaction may be partly a consequence my habitual tendency to see the skull beneath the skin. It's also possible that during my adolescence, one or another of the writers who visited my parents at our family's house—among them the American Studies scholar Stuart James, the novelist John Williams, and the poet Alan Stephens—pointed out the shadows in Frost's snowy landscape. In any case, I never felt inclined to see this poem as the dollop of maple syrup that many people believe it to be.

Frost himself struggled with its implications. Although he wrote the first draft quickly, the ending caused him considerable difficulty. Jay Parini, one of Frost's biographers, writes: "The whole poem may have come to Frost in a flash, but he had great trouble with the last stanza. It was some time before he thought of solving the problem by simply repeating the last line: 'And miles to go before I sleep.'" [7] Even early on, many readers caught the ambiguous but troubling implications that result from the repetition. Some raised the issue with Frost at public events, though "in countless readings of the poem in public, he would leave it open to the listener to decide what was meant by the poem's suggestive final stanza." Now and then he would be more explicit—and even reassuring. "To an audience at Bread Loaf," writes Parini, "he once said that the ominous-sounding last lines don't necessarily mean that 'you're going to do anything bad' when you get home." [8] Frost even took umbrage over suggestions that the final stanza suggests a longing for death. As late as 1962—the year before he died—Frost was still denying that thanatos suffuses the poem. The American poet Louise Bogan commented on a November reading that year: "He insisted that 'Stopping by Woods' was NOT concerned with Death . . . " [9]

My own belief is that the poem itself refutes Frost's denials. Another of Frost's biographers, Jeffrey Meyers, writes: "The theme of 'Stopping by Woods'—despite Frost's disclaimer—is the temptation of death, even suicide, symbolized by the woods that are filling up with snow on the darkest evening of the year. The speaker is powerfully drawn to these woods . . . and wants to lie down and let the snow cover and bury him. The third quatrain,

5

with its drowsy, dream-like line: 'Of easy wind and downy flake,' opposes the horse's instinctive urge for home and the man's subconscious desire for death in the dark, snowy woods. The speaker says, 'The woods are lovely, dark and deep,' but he resists their morbid attraction." [10]

Moreover, I believe that the darker aspect of the poem hinges on a single comma—or, rather, on the absence of one. The first line of the final stanza appears in two different ways in several different editions. *The Poetry of Robert Frost,* edited by Edward Connery Lathem, places a comma after "dark." [11] The mid-1990's Library of America edition deletes this comma. The presence or absence of that tiny punctuation mark subtly but profoundly changes the line's significance. "The woods are lovely, dark, and deep" presents the forest's attributes as loveliness, darkness, and deepness. "The woods are lovely, dark and deep" states both that the woods are lovely and that their loveliness consists of being dark and deep. The distinction isn't a question of pedantry but of existential substance. The critic Richard Poirier describes the situation bluntly: "In fact, the woods are not, as the Lathem edition would have it (with its obtuse emendation of a comma after the second adjective in line 13), merely 'lovely, dark, and deep.' Rather, as Frost in all the editions he supervised, they are 'lovely, [i.e.] dark and deep'; the loveliness thereby partakes of the depth and darkness which make the woods so ominous." [12]

Do that comma and its implications matter? In a world where almost two billion people lack sufficient food, where dozens of armed conflicts kill innocent civilians every day, where more than sixty million people are refugees, and where all inhabitants of the planet are threatened by climate disruption and environmental degradation, the obvious answer is No. Yet perhaps the comma (or its absence) are significant anyway—on a literary level, at least, and perhaps on other levels as well. I would suggest three reasons why.

First, because the comma or its absence reveal Frost for what he is—a writer far more interesting and complex than the benign, grandfatherly New England farmer often celebrated in popular

American culture. He is a writer whose portraits, both of the land and of people, reveal as much shadow as light.

Second, they matter because this poem, like others among Frost's finest poems, delivers an existential jolt. As Poirier states it neatly, "the woods are lovely and . . . their loveliness consists of being dark and deep." The shadows have their own magnetic pull. One can resist their pull; one ought to; but it's a mistake to deny the reality of this gravitational tug.

Third, they matter because ultimately this poem shows that the woods—their loveliness, darkness and deepness—aren't external.

Una Selva Oscura

> I am walking alone in a dark forest and I notice that
> I have lost my way.
>
> —C. G. Jung, *The Red Book* [13]

ntering the Dark Forest or the Enchanted Forest is a threshold symbol of the soul entering the perils of the unknown," writes J.C. Cooper in *An Illustrated Encyclopaedia of Traditional Symbols*. The forest is "the realm of death; the secrets of nature, or the spiritual world. . . . " In many folk tales, legends, and survival stories, the "[r]etreat into the forest is symbolic [of] death before initiatory rebirth." [14] Consistent with this view, the psychologist Bruno Bettelheim believed that wooded environments represent the inner realms of the mind. "Since ancient times the near impenetrable forest . . . has symbolized the dark, hidden, near-impenetrable world of our unconscious. [When] we succeed in finding our way out we . . . emerge with a much more highly developed humanity." [15] Stories about entering dark woods and struggling with strange experiences range from fairy tales ("Little Red Riding Hood," "Hansel and Gretel," "Vasilisa the Beautiful") to children's books (Frank Baum's *The Wonderful Wizard of Oz*, Gary Paulsen's *Hatchet*, and George MacDonald's *Phastastes*) to classical drama (Shakespeare's *A Midsummer Night's Dream*) to musical theater (Stephen Sondheim and James Lapine's *Into the Woods*) to canonic poems as varied as Dante's *Inferno* and Spenser's *The Faerie Queene*. [16]

Why is forest imagery so common, and what accounts for all the dark symbolism? Robert Pogue Harrison, writing in *Forests: The Shadow of Civilization,* an exploration of forests in Western thought and imagination, states that most inhabited lands throughout the West were more or less densely forested in the past. Western culture literally cleared its space in the midst of wooded places. The dark, densely vegetated areas thus defined the limits of civilization—the line between the Known and the Beyond. The forest has tended to represent "an outlying realm of opacity which has allowed . . . civilization to estrange itself, enchant itself, terrify itself . . . in short, to project into the forest shadows its secrets and innermost anxieties." Writing of the brothers Grimm, for instance, Harrison notes that

> Anyone familiar with the Grimms' fairy tales knows how prominently forests figure in the collection as a whole. These forests typically lie beyond the bounds of the familiar world. They are the places where protagonists get lost, meet unusual creatures, undergo spells and transformations, and confront their destinies. Children typically "grow up" during their ventures in the forests. The forests are sometimes places of the illicit—Little Red Riding Hood learns her lesson in the forest, telling herself at the end of the tale: "Never again will you stray from the path by yourself and go into the forest when your mother has forbidden it"—yet more often than not they are places of weird enchantment. [17]

Christian traditions, especially, have tended to view forests as symbolic of the Other. Harrison goes on to state that "The Christian Church . . . was essentially hostile toward this impassive frontier of unhumanized nature. Bestiality, fallenness, errancy, perdition—these are the associations that accrued around forests in the Christian mythology. In theological terms forests represented the anarchy of matter itself . . . " Culturally, they "represented for the Church the last strongholds of Pagan worship. The darkness of forests—full of dangerous beasts both real and imagined—stood in opposition to the light of divinity cast from above." Harrison adds that "Where divinity has been identified with the sky, or with the eternal geometry of the stars, or with the cosmic infinity, or with 'heaven,' the forests became monstrous." [18]

> As the underside of the ordained world, forests represented for the Church the last strongholds of pagan worship. In the tenebrous Celtic forests reigned the Druid priests; in the forests of Germany stood those sacred groves where unconverted barbarians engaged in heathen rituals; in the nocturnal forests at the edge of town sorcerers, alchemists, and all the tenacious survivors of paganism concocted their mischief. [19]

Beyond all these issues of European history, symbolism, theology, and tale-telling lurks a simple, more visceral aspect of the situation. Woods can be scary places. Straying off a forest path—straying literally, not symbolically—almost always inspires dismay, concern, dread, alarm, and even panic. Spending a night lost in the woods leads to a state of hypervigilance. Every rustle of the leaves inspires uncertainty and fear. Is that creaking noise just the wind in the branches . . . or is it a bear's approach? Uncertainty and fatigue leave the nerves jangled. Time slows to a crawl. Dawn seems eons distant. All of life's other problems shrink and vanish. As Walker Percy once noted: If you wish to cure yourself of modern existential angst, just spend a night lost in the bayou. You'll be eager—desperate—to trade the tangible, acute miseries and potentially life-threatening dangers of moment-by-moment survival for the familiar anxieties of contemporary life.

Not, Not, Not

ne late-November morning a few years ago, Edith and I visited the Robert Frost Stone House Museum, currently maintained by the Friends of Robert Frost, in South Shaftsbury, Vermont. We had stayed overnight in Bennington with intent to visit the Stone House early the next morning, all the better to avoid the schoolchildren who often tour the place on field trips. The parking lot was almost empty—a good sign for crowd-averse visitors like us. Then we noticed a small slate hung on a fence near the path to the house: CLOSED TODAY. The museum's website hadn't mentioned this disruption of the schedule, so how could we have known? Edith and I stood near the car for a while and discussed our options. We could come back some other time, of course . . . But South Shaftsbury is a two-and-a-half-hour drive from our town, so we weren't thrilled to contemplate making another trip. Maybe we could have a look anyway? We walked up to the house, spoke with some of the contractors whose renovations had prompted the closure, and got their permission to explore the grounds, at least.

The house, built circa 1769, is fairly unremarkable in appearance despite its age. Two stories tall, it has a stone front and gabled ends. Double windows flank the centered front door. There's a pointed dormer in front and a single, very wide dormer with three windows in back. Brick chimneys rise from each end of the roof. The main roof slants down to a long closed-in back porch with sashed windows and plaid curtains. The window trim throughout is maroon. The back door opens out onto a small, stone-bordered plot of grass, then a much larger lawn stretching out toward a big gray barn, a single large white birch, and the woods beyond. Circling the house, Edith and I peered in through the windows but couldn't see much, given the bright reflections on the window panes, and we didn't want to annoy the nearby workmen; then, feeling abashed to behave like a pair of literary peeping Toms, we left the house and walked west across the back lawn toward the line of trees.

It wasn't as if I had necessarily expected Frost's South Shaftsbury woods to be The Woods as described in his iconic poem. I hadn't even assumed that these woods were his inspiration. The forest he described in "Stopping by Woods" was a grove in his mind, not on his land. Even so, I wanted to see the property he had owned during his decade in South Shaftsbury. I wanted to walk among the trees that Frost might have gazed upon through his kitchen window as he wrote early one morning in June of 1922.

Edith and I walked down a grassy path—once a road, surely— that took us away from the Stone House and across its back lawn. Dilapidated stone walls bordered the path, with rough meadow grasses rising alongside the rocks. This path declined for a hundred yard until it reached the forest. The trees were bare of leaves. Maple and birch predominated, though I saw a few stout pines as well. What seemed most striking was the thorny underbrush. Brambles rose both to the left and the right along the path and deep into the forest. Walking off-trail would have been possible but not easy or fun; pushing through the thicket would have left us scratched and bleeding. Edith and I kept to the footpath, which was wide and even. We proceeded for several hundred yards. The trail angled to the right, then started to decline. Many of the trees ahead were damaged, with ragged limbs and fallen branches angled this way and that. We continued on the footpath, letting it take us gradually downward until it opened up rather quickly into . . . a swamp. I was struck at once by the unappealing nature of these woods—not lovely, not dark, not deep.

Treeness

n her memoir *Living with a Wild God*, Barbara Ehrenreich describes a series of experiences, including one occurring at the edge of a forest, that troubled her as a teenager.

I had wandered off and was leaning on a fence, staring at the woods in the pale late-summer sunlight, feeling nothing but impatience . . .

And then it happened. Something peeled off the visible world, taking with it all meaning, inference, association, and words. If anyone had asked, I would have said I was looking at a tree, but the word "tree" was gone, along with all the notions of treeness that had accumulated in the dozen or so years since I had acquired language. Was it a place that was suddenly revealed to me? Or was it a substance—the indivisible, elemental material out of which the entire known and agreed-upon world arises as a fantastic elaboration? I don't know, but I was alarmed to discover that when you take away all human attributions—the words, the names of species, the wisps of remembered tree-related poetry, the fables of photosynthesis and capillary action—that when you take all of this away, there is still something left.

I snapped out of it soon enough. . . . [20]

Driving home after the family excursion that afternoon, Ehrenreich settled in for the evening with her parents and sister. She ate dinner with her parents and sister, then withdrew to her room, where she read poetry until bedtime. "They were just doing their job, these poets, which is really the job of all of us—to keep applying coat upon coat of human passion and grandiosity to the world around us, trying to cover up whatever it is that lies underneath." She mused uneasily over what had taken place earlier that day. "I decided that evening that whatever I had experienced . . . had to be an aberration, like the retinal floaters that sometimes intruded on my vision after I'd been in the car too long on a hot, bright day. . . . Sleep deprivation does odd things to the mind, and this must be one of them, I thought—except it kept happening, and it gained legitimacy through repetition." After a sequence of these experiences in different settings over a period of several years, Ehrenreich struggled to interpret what had been happening. Eventually, she writes, "I came up with my own explanation, patched together from fragments of psychology I had picked up at the Lowell Public Library, which suggested that the most routine perception requires an impressive creative effort." The human sensory apparatus and the brain collaborate, she realized, not so much to perceive reality as to construct it. "There was plenty of input still pouring in as colors and lights and sound, but it wasn't getting sorted and categorized." She goes on to state that "There is a word for the episodes I was experiencing, though it was not available to me at the time: 'dissociation,' described in the psychiatric literature as 'feeling unreal' (either that one is unreal or that the world around one is unreal, if those two conditions can even be distinguished)." Describing this phenomenon as general cognitive breakdown, Ehrenreich then quotes the *Diagnostic and Statistical Manual of Mental Disorders* regarding "the disruption . . . in the normal integration of consciousness, memory, identity, emotion, [or] perception." And she comments about herself: "in other words, one of these areas is not working correctly." [21]

The American novelist Reynolds Price, writing in his memoir *Clear Pictures*, describes his own experience in a forest—a sense of relating to a forest. Living with his family at the time on the rural outskirts of Asheboro, North Carolina, Price spent long afternoons roaming through the woods. There, at the age of six, "with no knowledge of Wordsworth, Thoreau or the other pantheist nature poetry of England and America, I came upon a faith of my own, parallel to theirs but newly found."

> I wedged my hunting knife into the soft bark of a pine tree. I pressed my lips to the dull edge of the cool blade. In that moment as I felt the tree's life in the steel, I knew that the world beyond me—every separate thing that

was not Reynolds Price—was as alive as I. Through means that, then or now, I couldn't begin to explain, I knew that all matter was alive and aware—listening, seeing, hearing or feeling in its own way. . . . Every thing knew, or knew of, every other thing; and each understood its kinship with all. . . . I perceived an immense created being, dispersed in millions of things. And I worked to press myself toward the being. I wanted it to know me as fully as possible and for me to know it. [22]

Unlike Ehrenreich, who has described herself repeatedly and consistently as an atheist, Price framed his own experience as theistic from the start: "Since I'd heard a lot about God, I assumed God had made this single thing. But I knew God wasn't it—God was not a rock, and he surely wasn't me. He was watching us though, with hope and a set of powerful rules that I needed to learn. [23] At later stages of his life, Price both accepted and pulled back from his boyhood experience, and he refined his sense of what he had experienced.

When I moved out of my trees-and-rocks mysticism into my years of church religion, it took me a while to see that I'd done two sizable things. One was good; one was ultimately bad. . . . The good was a slow discovery that my early sense of the connection, the union, of all things could lead me to a serious error. Tempting as the notion of that union was . . . I ran a grave risk in thinking that all things were not only one thing but that each thing contained its rightful portion of God the maker. I'd almost believed we're made out of God, and that's as risky an error as any. [24]

❧   ❧   ❧

The Romantic movement, both in England and elsewhere in Europe, included beliefs that would have rejected the notion that being "made out of God" was "as risky an error as any other."

Wordsworth, Coleridge, and Shelley in England all subscribed to variants of what Coleridge called "the latency of all in each." Similar pantheistic beliefs held true for Goethe in Germany and, later, for Whitman in America: beliefs that the Universe or Nature as the totality of everything is identical with divinity, as well as beliefs that an immanent God suffuses Nature or the Universe. None of these ideas was new. They are prominent in the early Vedas, in some aspects of ancient Egyptian religion, in some of the Presocratics, in some of the Stoics (starting with Zeno of Citium), in Marcus Aurelius, and in some of the early Gnostic Christian groups. During the Renaissance, Giordano Bruno espoused the concept of an immanent and infinite God—a heresy against Catholic doctrine that contributed to his excommunication and to his being burned at the stake in 1600. The most prominent pre-modern exponent of pantheism, however, was Baruch Spinoza, whose *Ethics* countered Descartes' emphatic dualism—the belief that the body and spirit are completely separate. By contrast, Spinoza held that body and spirit are the same, and he regarded God as the unity of all substance. (This concept led to Spinoza's own excommunication from the Jewish community in Amsterdam.) Pantheism gained adherents in the eighteenth century and eventually found widespread expression among the Romantics throughout Europe.

Wordsworth, writing in "Lines Written a Few Miles above Tintern Abbey," expresses these beliefs emphatically and eloquently:

> . . . And I have felt
> A presence that disturbs me with the joy
> Of elevated thoughts; a sense sublime
> Of something far more deeply interfused,
> Whose dwelling is the light of setting suns,
> And the round ocean, and the living air,
> And the blue sky, and in the mind of man,
> A motion and a spirit, that impels
> All thinking things, all objects of all thought,

> And rolls through all things. Therefore am I still
> A lover of the meadows and the woods . . .[25]

Therefore am I still / A lover of the meadows and the woods . . . The "presence" inherent "in all things"—Coleridge's "the latency of all in each"—is the immanent God coexistent and coequal with Nature. As H. W. Piper describes the situation: "One of the most prominent features of English Romantic thought is the belief that the universe was a living unity . . . [,] the belief that this life could be found in each natural object and that, through the imagination, a real communication was possible between man and the forms of nature." [26] Wordsworth doesn't describe a tree as such in "Tintern Abbey." If young William had confronted an individual tree in the same way that Ehrenreich and Price did during their respective youths, I find it hard to believe that he wouldn't have perceived it as a manifestation of the imminent God.

Unmedi(t)ated Experience

> "[M]editation empties mind of words, concepts, and stories, the preoccupations that distance us from the immediate presence of earth's ten thousand things."
>
> —David Hinton, *Hunger Mountain* [27]

arbara Ehrenreich, writing about her unnerving adolescent experience, states that while staring at the woods, she found that "[s]omething peeled off the visible world, taking with it all meaning, inference, association, and words." She decided later that same day that "whatever I had experienced . . . had to be an aberration"; and, later still, she concluded that this experience was the result of dissociation—a pathological state. But what if Ehrenreich's experience—"looking at a tree, but [with] the word "tree" . . . gone, along with all the notions of treeness that had accumulated in the dozen or so years since I had acquired language"—what if this experience isn't necessarily dissociation but, instead connection? Perhaps "taking [away] all meaning, inference, association, and words" isn't necessarily a psychiatric aberration but, instead (at least under some conditions), a normal and rich experience. An experience that, far from isolating the person who undergoes it, returns her to the ground of her being. The question I'm raising here brings us to the Buddhist concept of "unmediated experience." Is it possible that the human sensorium, in collaboration with the human mind, can perceive objects, events, and experiences without the trappings of "meaning, inference, association, and words," as Ehrenreich puts it? That is, can a person experience the world itself rather than a heavily filtered, interpreted, potentially distorted view of the world? Attempting to answer these questions can benefit from considering the Buddhist concept of mindfulness (in Pali: *sati*, also translated as "bare attention").

First, however, an aside—and a caveat. Over the past ten or fifteen years, the concept of mindfulness has been extracted from the realm of Buddhist philosophy and meditation and has been adapted to an almost infinite array of mainstream purposes. Or, to put the situation more bluntly, mindfulness has been kidnapped from the meditation hall and put to work in the marketplace. You can now attend workshops on mindfulness is schools, churches, and storefronts throughout the land. You can buy DVDs, online courses, and iPhone apps to teach you mindfulness. Medical clinics teach mindfulness to help patients manage chronic pain. Psychologists teach mindfulness to help clients ease anxiety and depression. Corporations teach mindfulness to help sales reps, assembly line workers, managers, and executives cope with workplace stress, increase productivity, and achieve organizational goals. Several branches of the U.S. military teach mindfulness to help soldiers reduce stress and focus on their duties. In short, non-Buddhists have adopted and commodified mindfulness in a thousand different ways.

Some benefits may accrue from this phenomenon. However, even a cursory review of this commodification warrants concern.

More traditional Buddhists are concerned that mindfulness has been co-opted, diluted, and cheapened. At the same time, some non-Buddhist observers feel concerned that if mindfulness can be so easily adapted to such varied and sometimes questionable purposes, perhaps it doesn't have much going for it after all. These are legitimate concerns. I can understand the sources of the backlash currently developing against the fad of mindfulness. I sympathize with a thoughtful friend of mind who exclaimed, "I'm sick of all this mindfulness!" At the same time, I believe that rejecting the fundamental Buddhist concept and practice of *sati* on account of faddish spinoffs is like bulldozing a lush, vibrant orange grove because you hold Tang in contempt.

Returning to the main point, however: the concept of mindfulness may clarify Ehrenreich's experience and its implications.

Here's how a prominent Buddhist monk and teacher, Bhante Guranatana, describes the nature and value of mindfulness:

> When you first become aware of something, there is a fleeting instant pure awareness just before you conceptualize the thing, before you identify it. That is a state of awareness. Ordinarily, this state is short-lived. It is that flashing split second just as you focus your eyes on the thing, just as you focus your mind on the thing, just before you objectify it, clamp down on it mentally, and segregate it from the rest of existence. . . . That flowing, soft-focus moment of pure awareness is mindfulness. In that brief flashing mind-moment you experience a thing as an un-thing. You experience a softly flowing moment of pure experience that is interlocked with the rest of reality, not separate from it. . . . [T]his moment of soft, unfocused awareness contains a very deep sort of knowing that is lost as soon as you focus your mind and objectify the object into a thing. In the process of ordinary perception, the mindfulness step is so fleeting as to be unobservable. We have developed a habit

of squandering our attention on all remaining steps, focusing on the perception, cognizing the perception, labeling it, and most of all, getting involved in a long string of symbolic thought about it. That original moment of mindfulness is rapidly passed over. [28]

Guranatana further clarifies the nature of mindfulness by describing these attributes [with my italics]:

Mindfulness is pre-symbolic. It is not shackled to logic.

Mindfulness is not intellectual awareness. It is just aware.

Mindfulness is participatory observation. The meditator is both participant and observer at one and the same time.

Mindfulness is mirror-thought. It reflects only what is presently happening and in exactly the way it is happening.

Mindfulness is nonjudgmental observation. It is the ability of the mind to observe without criticism. It does not take sides. It does not get hung up on what is perceived. It just perceives.

Mindfulness is non-conceptual awareness. . . . It is not thinking. It does not get involved with thoughts or concepts. It does not get hung up on ideas or opinions or memories.

Mindfulness registers experiences, but it does not compare them. It does not label or categorize them. It just observes everything. It is . . . the direct and immediate experiencing of whatever is happening, without the medium of thought. It comes before thought in the perceptual process.

Mindfulness is present-time awareness. It takes place in the here and now. It is the observance of what is happening right now, in the present moment.

Mindfulness is non-egotistic alertness. It takes place without reference to self. With mindfulness one sees all phenomena without references to concepts like "me," "my," or "mine."

Mindfulness is awareness of change. It is observing the passing flow of experience. It is watching things as they are changing. Mindfulness is watching things moment by moment, continuously.

Mindfulness is objective, but it is not cold or unfeeling. It is the wakeful experience of life, an alert participation in the ongoing process of living.

Mindfulness adds nothing to perception and it subtracts nothing. It distorts nothing. It is bare attention and just looks at whatever comes up. [28]

To summarize: *sati,* mindfulness, is a state of awareness. It's now widely understood even outside of the Buddhist community that mindfulness involves being "in the moment." However, mindfulness isn't only a matter of being in the moment. Most central and most important to *sati* is what one does with the moment. The goal is a full waking awareness of whatever is happening. As the American Buddhist writer Joseph Goldstein writes in his description of sati: "Bare attention . . . brings the mind to a state of rest. Bare attention means observing things as they are." [29]

Revisiting Ehrenreich's account of her unsettling adolescent experience, it's worth noting her succinct description: "I would have said I was looking at a tree, but the word "tree" was gone, along with all the notions of treeness that had accumulated in the dozen or so years since I had acquired language." Viewed from a Buddhist perspective, it appears that Ehrenreich experienced a state of precocious, unbidden, involuntary mindfulness. Every aspect of what she describes here coincides with Buddhist assumptions about *sati*—bare attention. This experience is vivid, intense, fundamental, and stripped of the assumptions, biases, memories, fantasies, and intellectual frameworks that can be rich in their own right but that also filter and even obstruct our perceptions. How and why did Ehrenreich's state of bare attention arise? That wasn't clear to her at the time, and she remained uncertain about its sources for a long time afterwards; otherwise she wouldn't have spent the next several decades attempting to make sense of what happened. What she describes, however, fits the description of what occurs during moments of intense mindfulness. Ehrenreich found this event disquieting, even alarming. States of unease and alarm aren't inevitable during meditation or under other circumstances conducive to mindfulness, but neither are they uncommon. Mindfulness strips away the habits of perception that prompt us to take the world for granted. Mindfulness removes the familiar context from the objects, events, thoughts, and emotions we perceive. As Ehrenreich succinctly states, "Something peeled off the visible world, taking with it all meaning, inference, association, and words." Mindfulness was the peeler. What remained after the process of peeling was (in Buddhist parlance) unmediated experience. Ehrenreich saw a tree, but she saw the tree [with] the word "tree" . . . gone, along with all the notions of treeness that had accumulated. The result was profoundly unsettling: "I was alarmed to discover that when you take away all human attributions—the words, the names of species, the wisps of remembered tree-related poetry, the fables of photosynthesis and capillary action—that when you take all of this away, there is still something left."

Or, to paraphrase Gertrude Stein's famous dictum: A tree is a tree is a tree.

This situation immediately drops us into deep waters: the question of what constitutes perception. For many years I've repeatedly mulled over Immanuel Kant's notion of *das Ding an sich*. This phrase is most commonly translated into English as "the thing in itself" or "the thing as such." What would it mean to perceive *das Ding an sich*? Given the nature of the human sensorium, would a perception of any *Ding an sich* even be possible? Stated another way: can I perceive something by a means (any means) that bypasses the senses I'm equipped with? The answer seems an obvious No. Since I'm a human being, the only way by which I can perceive anything is through the ordinary human senses. My senses necessarily keep me at a distance from what I perceive. [30]

Suppose that while walking in the woods, I notice a tree several hundred yards away. The tree suddenly falls over. I observe the trunk strike the ground and, just an instant later, I hear the crash. Which perception—the sight or the sound of the tree falling or the resulting crash—is the actual *event* of the tree's fall? The answer: neither one. Light travels faster than sound, so initially I saw the tree strike the ground; then, once the sound waves reached my ears after a brief lag, I heard the crash. But both sensory impressions were my delayed experience of an event that was already over before I "perceived" it. The same circumstances would hold true even if I perceived a stationary tree over a longer period time— for instance, by staring at or even meditating upon the tree. Try as I might, I would only experience my sensory impressions of the tree; I would never perceive *das Baum an sich*.

Is it possible, however, that under some circumstances I might perceive the tree in a less cluttered way—that is, through a less obtrusive filter of "meaning, inference, associations, and words"? This possibility is where *sati* enters the picture. By means of bare attention, I might attain a state of openness and clarity—what some schools of Buddhism call Big Mind—that would allow me something closer to a perceiving the tree itself rather than the tree festooned with the preconceptions, memories, emotions, attitudes, biases, preferences, aversions, and fantasies that I would habitually and unconsciously impose on it otherwise. That perception might lead to (or at least be part of) a more complete apprehension of the world than if I insist on imposing my own grab bag of impressions and preferences. While I might not perceive "the tree in itself," I might come closer to perceiving the tree more clearly, more fully, and in a less distorted way. Or, as the English literary critic John Banville states the situation: "Entire mythologies, entire theogonies, have been invented to shore up our manifold illusions. Human creatures pass their days in gloriously irresponsible denial of the cold reality staring them pitilessly in the face. . . . [T]he only solution must be to turn back to the thing, the *Ding* if not quite the *Ding an sich,* and refuse to be distracted by mere chattering: the thing, that is, and not our notions of it." [31]

Many years ago, a friend who practiced a form of meditation similar to my own told me, "What we're trying to do while meditating is to observe the world like babies—to see things as if for the first time. But we're trying to do that consciously." I resisted this notion at the time. As a twenty-four-year-old, I resented the possibility that babies might be more perceptive than I was in the full flower of young manhood. In my late sixties now, after having helped to raise a daughter and a son from birth through young adulthood, I can grasp and accept the wisdom of children—including babies. They do indeed see the world for the first time. The downside of their perceptions is lacking the context that years of experience allows. Perhaps, then, the benefit of mindfulness is to see the world as if for the first time but in a state of full, volitional, wakeful consciousness.

Whose Woods These Are I Think I Know

ne afternoon in late spring I start meditating in the woods. There's no hut down there, not even a crude platform, only a folding metal chair that I carried in the first time around and then abandoned among the maples for future use. It's easy to cross the meadow, enter the forest, find the chair, do my sitting, and leave.

Whenever I descend to that meditation place, I'm struck time after time that the woods are indeed lovely, dark, and deep—and also lovely, dark and deep. This place is just a few hundred yards from the house yet is a realm apart. Unlike our meadow, the forest can't be taken in at a glance; it can't be grasped. I walk among the trees but can see only fifty or a hundred feet ahead, often less. Overall, this isn't a dangerous place. I can't become literally lost in this Dark Wood—it's too small. A one-minute walk west and I'm back in the meadow. Our woods lack the sheer scope of the forested landscapes I've faced in the Rockies, the Olympics, and the Andes. While it's true that wild animals live here—the fox, coyote, deer, moose, bear whose tracks Edith and I have seen—these creatures generally keep their distance. Something jolts in a nearby tree, and I startle . . . but the marauding beast is only a blue jay. No, the creatures aren't a menace. What's alarming in the woods is what's alrming anywhere: the otherness of the Other. Only in this sense am I playing with fire. How great is the risk? Hard to say. Connect with that power and I may as well grab a high-voltage wire. What will I do, then, if the woods truly reveal themselves—if they overturn my comfortable assumptions that the tree trunks, the branches, the twigs, the leaves, the birds, and the scraps of sky visible overhead are only the beautiful surfaces they present to me?

Even so, meditating in the woods quickly becomes a routine that I enjoy and deeply value.

The woods in springtime . . .

The bare branches are budding. Sunlight remains weak but still manages to penetrate the sparse foliage. The breeze plays the tiny leaves: a stretto fugue of rustles. Phoebes call out in intervals of descending minor seconds. Meditation in this setting is so easy that it's difficult: there's a constant risk of falling asleep. I try my best to stay alert. Almost at once, however, I doze off and immediately plunge into REM sleep. My dream: sitting in these same woods and fretting about my recent diagnosis of sleep apnea. I perceive myself recalling the initial consultation with the somnologist, my overnight sleep study at the medical center, and the follow-up visit with the doctor, who informs me: *We have many treatment options.* My eyes snap open. I'm bewildered to find myself not in the doctor's office but in a forest. For a moment, everything I see around me is black-and-white. Last year's leaves lie at my feet, a few fallen branches among them, and stick-like maple saplings rise before me.

The woods in summer . . .

Full foliage now, deep green drenched in shadow. Not just the canopy but the underbrush, too, is fully leafed, blocking my view beyond half a dozen yards. Birdsong is continuous: the sparrows' twitters, the jays' shrieks, the crows' caws, the robins' exclamations, and, late each afternoon, the wood thrushes' liquid notes. Beyond the birds I hear the wind in the trees: cyclical, heavy, surf-like. The air is warm enough to feel like an embrace, so I'm comfortable and feel no distractions from my own body. It's hard to avoid feeling that this place is perfect. Time slows and stops. There is nowhere else on earth.

The woods in autumn . . .

This fall has been the most colorful that Edith and I have experienced so far. The leaves started turning early, stoked to incendiary reds and oranges, and stayed brilliant much longer than usual. Why? We had an unseasonable cold spell in late September—temps in the low twenties—so perhaps the hard frost jump-started the colors. Beyond that, who knows. The consequences for me are a meditation spot that stays temperate and radiant a week into November. Sitting in the woods is effortless and serene. As the leaves fall, clicking and clattering around me, the sunlight intensifies day by day. Soon I'm basking in warm, yellow light even in the middle of the woods.

My question day after day, week after week, month after month, season after season: to what degree does meditating here reveal the woods at all . . . or does sitting here reveal only more layers of my thoughts and feelings about the woods?

A tree is a tree is a tree. The woods are the woods are the woods.

The Longest Evening of the Year

> His soul swooned slowly as he heard the snow falling faintly through the universe and faintly falling, like the descent of their last end, upon all the living and the dead.
>
> —James Joyce, "The Dead" [32]

n the winter solstice I venture down the hillside to my meditation spot. This part of the forest was open land throughout most of the 19th century; the Whitcombs, the family who built our house in 1840, surely grazed their sheep here. Now the slope is fully wooded. I arrive here at just past four in the afternoon, but the light is already fading. This is the longest evening of the year. We've had such heavy snowfall in recent weeks that I'm startled to grasp today as only the first day of winter. A layer of snow almost two feet thick blankets the ground. I haven't come here in over two weeks, so I locate my meditation chair only after several minutes of probing with a trekking pole. I tug it out, dust it off, and shove the legs back into the snowy substrate. I have to clear a space in front of the chair so that my legs have a place to rest. These preparations make for an awkward start. Yet despite the stark setting and the chilly air— it's eighteen degrees out—I'm intent on meditating here. I've prepared by wearing long johns, a turtleneck shirt, a sweater, a fleece, a parka, insulated boots, and ski mittens. I sit and settle in.

Light snowfall sifts through the trees. When I look straight up, I notice tiny clusters of flakes spiraling toward me. Their impact on my face feels lighter than the touch of gnats in summertime. The sky above is ashen. All around I see countless dark twigs, each one sheathed in ice from last week's storm, the ice in turn coated with snow from a few days ago. The almost total lack of wind leaves the snow intact. There must be some kind of breeze jostling the upper reaches of the trees, however, because I hear not so much a hiss as an intricate rustle like that of a hundred thousand shreds of cellophane being crumpled and uncrumpled. I sit as I always sit. I watch my breath in the usual way. After the effort of slogging down here and digging out the chair, I need a few minutes before I can settle down and settle in. Our property is almost always peaceful, and this little spot deep within the woods offers peace within the peace. Soon I grow calm.

Then a recurrent worry surfaces: how alone am I here, anyway? Sportsmen sometimes venture onto our land. The various hunting seasons are now long over, so the presence of intruders is unlikely. (Just to be safe, I've worn my day-glo orange pullover cap to avoid the possibility that an off-season "jack hunter" might somehow mistake a meditating Buddhist for a deer.) If not people, what about animals? The local bear is surely hibernating ... but maybe not, since climate change has thrown many large mammals' winter patterns off schedule. What will happen if I see her loom through the snowfall and approach me? How eager will I be to have an unmediated experience of nature? To grasp *die Bär an sich?* Or, more likely, to be grasped by her? No thanks. Sitting there, I'm relieved when it's clear that our neighborhood *Ursus americanus* won't bother to visit. I'm relieved, too, when I receive no attention from *das Fuchs an sich, das Wolf an sich,* or *das Elchbulle an sich*—although neighbors have recently mentioned spotting a fox, a wolf, and a moose in the area. I'm here alone. Except for the hiss of snowflakes all around me, nothing moves or makes a sound.

I sit for a long time. Nothing happens. As seems typical of my meditation, I reach no insight. Or perhaps the insight is simply that I've reached no insight. I'm here. That's it. That's all.

What, exactly, am I expecting? What am I trying to accomplish? Do I hope that by sitting among the trees I may feel something like what Barbara Ehrenreich felt when she found the word "tree" gone, along with all the notions of treeness that had accumulated over the years, yet still discovered something left over? Or am I hoping to perceive, as Reynolds Price appears to have concluded, that if all things "were not only one thing, [with] each thing [containing] its rightful portion of God the Maker," then there's an unbridgeable gap between God and Creation? Or am I hoping that, like the young Wordsworth, I might perceive "a sense sublime / Of something far more deeply interfused, . . . / . . . [that] rolls through all things"?

What would any of these perceptions tell me? If I could look at the woods and fully experience their loveliness, darkness, and deepness, what would I perceive?

Would I perceive that

$$God = Nature$$
$$and$$
$$Nature = God$$

and that for this reason the forest itself, as part of Nature, harbors some portion of divinity?

Would I perceive that

$$God \neq Nature$$
$$and$$
$$Nature \neq God$$

and in fact that God and Nature lie on opposite sides of a chasm—that God is the Creator and Nature is the altogether separate and subordinate Creation? And that as a tiny mote within Creation, I can perceive the splendor of what lies around me but never perceive the Creator as such?

Or would I perceive that

$$nature = nature = nature$$

and nothing more—that the woods are devoid of any divine substance and equally devoid of a Creator's mark—that is, that the trees are the trees, the forest is the forest, the snow is the snow, end of story?

Perhaps this is why the woods—lovely, dark and deep—inspire both longing and dread. The woods are beautiful indeed. If perceived clearly, however, they are vast, unfathomable, non-human, soulless. They have the potential to absorb without a trace anyone who, entering their realm, doesn't step carefully. Yet the woods' vastness and beauty are precisely what often draw me into them.

Sitting there and starting to shiver, I can't answer my own questions. In fact, I can't even ask the questions any more clearly than I have in the past—less so, perhaps, since I'm now growing more uncomfortable with each passing moment.

I'm disappointed but not surprised. What do I expect, really, coming down here to meditate in eighteen-degree weather? Enough already. Time to quit. Time to cover my chair with the black garbage bag I use to protect it and trudge up the hillside back to the house.

Then, unbidden, a strange interlude. While sitting there with my eyes closed, I watch the blankness of my shut-down field of vision open up and erupt into clouds of light. I say clouds because what I see appears almost meteorological in its scope and intensity, much as I've watched thunderheads billow toward me above timberline while hiking in the Rockies. The light is somehow both orange-pink and pale blue. It simultaneously unfolds before me and washes over me. My first thought is that sunlight striking my face has triggered this phenomenon. But I'm facing east, the sun has already set at my back, and dusk is deepening into nightfall. When I open my eyes, everything before me is darker than when my eyes are closed. The light resumes fulminating when I close them again. The sight is both dazzling and subtle, at once voluptuous and insubstantial. It's so lovely that I can't stop watching. I've seen this brilliance before, though not in recent years. It's always a delight, always marvelous. What does it mean? Probably nothing. Is it . . . significant? Unlikely. The meditation teachers I've studied with, as well as many Buddhist writers whose books I've read, all state that no matter how impressive and enjoyable such experiences, they aren't important and may even be risky. Why? Because they are distractions and potential stumbling blocks. Like all thoughts, emotions, and experiences that arise during meditation, they are best simply observed and allowed to pass. For this reason I observe what's before me, I steep in this billowing cloud, and I let it diminish and fade away. [33]

By now I'm engulfed in slate-gray dusk. I could stay in the woods and accomplish little beyond getting chilled. If I persist, I'll suffer acute hypothermia. How long will it take before I experience confusion, decreased heart rate, metabolic shutdown, respiratory failure, and cardiac arrest? These are the outcomes that Frost's protagonist would have faced if he had abandoned his sleigh, entered the woods, and allowed the forest to absorb him. What would he have gained by doing so? Perhaps a realization of being a thread in the fabric of nature, fully interwoven as part of the tapestry yet also insignificant and transitory. A worthwhile insight. However, gaining it at the cost of death by exposure isn't what I have in mind. Meditating here is perfect, calm, serene—the only sound's the sweep of easy wind and downy flake—but after another ten minutes I've had enough. I want to go inside. I want to be back in the house with the lights on and a fire in the woodstove. I want to fix dinner for Edith and our son and our daughter, Cory and Robin, who are visiting for the holidays. I want to sit with them, share the meal, and enjoy the warmth of their companionship. *Sati*—bare attention? I want that too. *Bodhi*—full waking consciousness? Maybe I'll attain that some day as well—and, who knows, maybe even while sitting in our little forest. Not tonight, though. Not here.

The woods are lovely . . . dark . . . opaque . . .
But I have promises to make,
And miles to go before I wake.
And miles to go before I wake.

Notes

[1] Dante Alighieri. *Inferno*. Robert Hollander and Jean Hollander, translators. New York: Doubleday, 2000. Citation: p. 3.

[2] Longfellow, Henry Wadsworth. *Evangeline*. Mineola, N.Y.: Dover Publications, 1995. Citation: p. 11.

[3] Snodgrass, W. D., quoted in Jeffrey Meyers, *Robert Frost: A Biography*. Boston: Houghton Mifflin, 1996. Citation: p. 184.

[4] Mertins, Louis. *Robert Frost: Life and Talks-Walking*. Norman, Oklahoma: University of Oklahoma Press, 1965. Citation: pp. 81-82.

[5] Tuten, Nancy Lewis; John Zubizarreta, *The Robert Frost Encyclopedia* (Santa Barbara, Calif.: Greenwood Publishing, 2001). Citation: p. 347.

[6] Frost, Robert. "Stopping by Woods on a Snowy Evening" in *Robert Frost: Collected Poems, Prose, and Plays*. Richard Poirier and Mark Richardson, eds. New York: Library of America, 1995.

[7] Parini, Jay. *Robert Frost: A Life*. New York: Henry Holt and Company, 1999. Citation: p. 208.

[8] Ibid., pp. 212-213.

[9] Meyers, op. cit., p. 327.

[10] Ibid., p. 180.

[11] Frost, *The Poetry of Robert Frost*, Edward Connery Lethem, ed. New York: Henry Holt and Company, 1969. page 224.

[12] Richard Poirier, *Robert Frost: The Work of Knowing.* London: Oxford University Press. Citation: p. 181.

[13] Jung, C. G. *The Red Book.* New York: W. W. Norton & Co., 2009. Citation: p. 261.

[14] Cooper, J. C. *An Illustrated Encyclopaedia of Traditional Symbols.* New York: Thames & Hudson, 1987. Citation: p. 287.

[15] Bruno Bettelheim, *The Uses Of Enchantment: The Meaning and Importance of Fairy Tales.* New York: Vintage Books, 2010. Citation: p. 112.

[16] A striking but not unique instance of how the Christian imagination can conflate actual woods with a dangerous spiritual landscape appears in Nathaniel Hawthorne's description of forests in *The Scarlet Letter.* Typical is this passage in Chapter 16, "A Forest Walk":

> The road, after the two wayfarers had crossed from the peninsula to the mainland, was no other than a footpath. It straggled onward into the mystery of the primeval forest. This hemmed it in so narrowly, and stood so black and dense on either side, and disclosed such imperfect glimpses of the sky above, that, to Hester's mind, it imaged not amiss the moral wilderness in which she had so long been wandering.

Hawthorne, Nathaniel. *The Scarlet Letter.* New York: Penguin Classics, 1962, 2016. Citation: p. 170.

[17] Harrison, William Pogue. *Forests: The Shadow of Civilization.* Chicago: University of Chicago Press, 1993. Citation: p. 169.

[18] Ibid., pp. 171.

[19] Ibid., pp. 61-62.

[20] Ehrenreich, Barbara. *Living with a Wild God: A Nonbeliever's Search for the Truth about Everything.* New York: Grand Central Publishing, 2014. Citation: pp. 47-48.

[21] Ibid., p. 53.

[22] Price, Reynolds. *Clear Pictures*. New York: Scribner, 2009. Citation: pp. 234-235.

[23] Ibid., pp. 235-236.

[24] Ibid., pp. 234-235.

[25] William Wordsworth, "Lines Written a Few Miles above Tintern Abbey," from *William Wordsworth,* Stephen Gill, ed., in *The Oxford Authors*. Oxford and New York: Oxford University Press, 1984, p. 134.

[26] Piper, H. W. *The Active Universe: Pantheism and the Concept of Imagination in the English Romantic Poets*. London: University of London, Athlone Press, 1961. Citation: pp. 3-4.

It's worth noting, however, that Wordsworth shifted his beliefs late in life to adopt a much more conventional, dualistic Christian framework for perceiving God and nature.

[27] Hinton, David. *Hunger Mountain*. Boulder, Colo.: Shambala, 2012. Citation: p. 9.

[28] Guranatana, Bhante. "Mindfulness" in *Voices of Insight,* Sharon Salzberg, ed. (Boston and London: Shambhala, 2001). Citation: pp. 133-139.

[29] Goldstein, Joseph. *The Experience of Insight: A Simple and Direct Guide to Buddhist Meditation*. (Boston and London: Shambhala, 1987). Citation: pp. 20-21.

[30] Kant, Immanuel. *Critique of Pure Reason;* ed. by Paul Guyer and Allen W. Wood. Cambridge: Cambridge University Press, 1999. Citation: pp. 338-345.

[31] Banville, John. "A Beautiful and Closely Woven Tapestry," in *The New York Review of Books,* Vol. LXII, No. 17 (November 5, 2015). Citation: page 60.

[32] Joyce, James. "The Dead" in *Dubliners.* New York: The Viking Press, Inc., 1967. Citation: p. 224.

[33] I've been intrigued for many years by how often this same phenomenon appears in the spiritual literature of many different traditions. Just one example: Augustine of Hippo writing in Book VII, Chapter 10, of *The Confessions:*

> I entered into the innermost part of myself. . . and I saw with my soul's eye (such as it was) an unchangeable light shining above this eye of my soul and above my mind. It was not the ordinary light which is visible to all flesh, nor something of the same sort, only bigger, as though it might be our ordinary light shining much more brightly and filling everything with greatness. No, it was not like that; it was different, entirely different from anything of the kind.

St. Augustine. *Confessions.* New York: New American Library, 1963. Citation: p. 149.

About the Author

Born in Denver and raised in Colorado, Mexico, and Peru, E. J. Myers attended Grinnell College and the University of Denver. He has worked in a wide variety of professions and trades, including inpatient health care, emergency medical services, carpentry, cabinetmaking, and publishing. He is the author of more than three dozen books, most published by mainstream companies, among them three novels (*The Mountain Made of Light, Fire and Ice,* and *The Summit*); fourteen children's books; and a well-received, much-reprinted book about bereavement, *When Parents Die: A Guide for Adults.* He has also co-authored or ghostwritten over a dozen books for clients or other authors. He lives with his wife in central Vermont.

For information about E. J. Myers, visit his Web site at:

www.edwardmyerswriter.net

About Montemayor Press

Montemayor Press is an independent publisher of literature for children and adults. To learn more about our books, visit:

www.MontemayorPress.com

or write for a catalogue at:

Montemayor Press
P. O. Box 546
Montpelier, VT 05601